Pippa and Pop

British English

Colin Sage

with Caroline Nixon & Michael Tomlinson

CAMBRIDGE
UNIVERSITY PRESS

Map of the book

	VOCABULARY	LANGUAGE	SOUNDS AND LETTERS	LITERACY AND VALUE	NUMBERS	CROSS-CURRICULAR
Introduction Page 4						
1 My friends Page 6	Hello Pippa, Pop, Dan, Kim book, crayon, pencil	Hello. I'm (Pippa). What's this? It's a (pencil).	Distinguishing sounds	Duck's friend Be friendly	Numbers: 1, 2	Social studies: Sharing
2 My family Page 18	brother, sister, daddy, mummy boy, girl, man, woman	She's the (mummy). He's my (brother). He's / She's a (boy).	Distinguishing sounds	The big carrot Help your family	Numbers: 3, 4	Science: How food grows
3 My toys Page 30	ball, doll, teddy, train blue, brown, red, yellow	It's a (ball). It's (red).	Distinguishing between letters and objects	Big teddy, small teddy Celebrate differences	Recognising patterns	Maths: Big and small
Units 1–3 Review Pages 42-43						
4 My body Page 44	ears, eyes, mouth, nose arms, feet, hands, legs	Touch your (nose). Colour the (arms).	Distinguishing between letters and numbers	Bunny's family Be kind	Recognising patterns	Social studies: Feelings

		VOCABULARY	LANGUAGE	SOUNDS AND LETTERS	LITERACY AND VALUE	NUMBERS	CROSS-CURRICULAR
5	**Food** Page 56	apples, bananas, biscuits, sandwiches / juice, milk, water	I like (apples). / I don't like (juice).	The letter sound a	Picky Peter / Say thank you	Numbers: 5, 6	Science: Identifying fruit
6	**Animals** Page 68	cat, dog, fish, rabbit / chair, table; on, under	Where's the (cat)? / Here it is. / It's (under) the (chair).	The letter sound e	Emma's new cat / Be kind to animals	Numbers: 7, 8	Science: What animals need
Units 4–6 Review Pages 80-81							
7	**Clothes** Page 82	hat, jacket, shoes, socks / dress, skirt, trousers, T-shirt	(Put on / Take off) your (hat). / I've got (a dress).	The letter sound i	Tommy's T-shirt / Be considerate	Shapes: circle, square, triangle	Art: Rough and smooth
8	**Transport** Page 94	bike, bus, car, van / drive a car, jump, ride a bike, run	I can see a (car). / I can (ride a bike).	The letter sound o	The hare and the tortoise / Be careful	Numbers: 9, 10	Science: Fast and slow
9	**The park** Page 106	bird, flower, frog, tree; green, pink / butterflies, caterpillars, ladybirds, worms	A (green) (tree). / What are these? / They're (butterflies).	The letter sound u	Penny in the park / Look after nature	One more	Maths: Symmetry
Units 7–9 Review Pages 118-119							

Welcome

👁 Look. 🔍 Find. ⭕ Trace. 💬 Say.

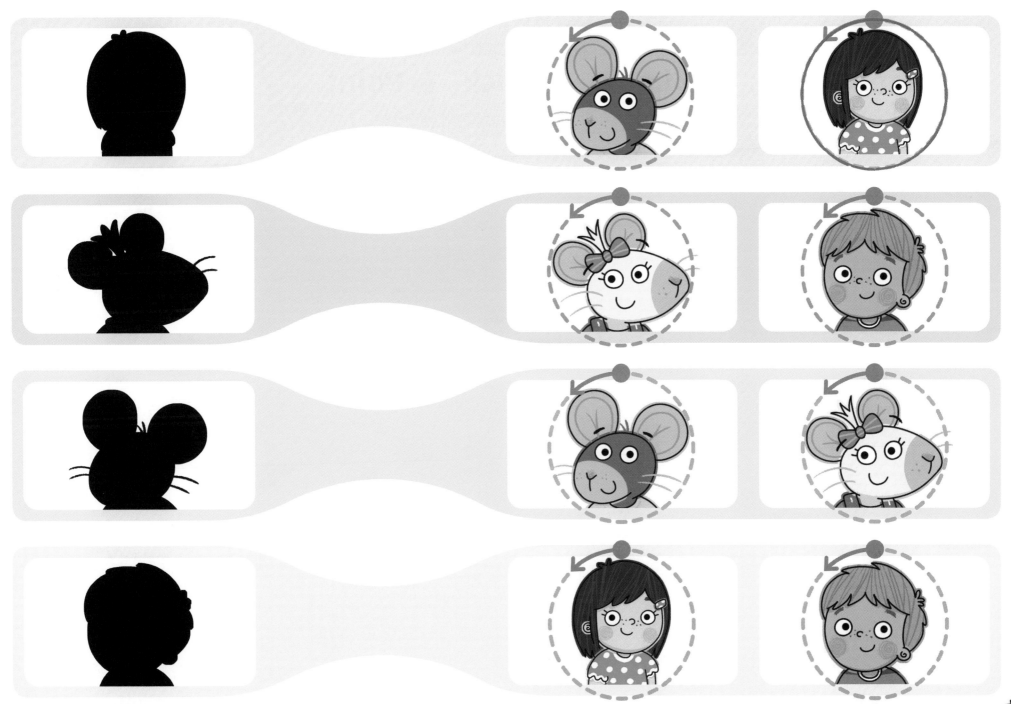

1 My friends

🎧³ Listen again. 👁 Look. 💬 Stick. ☝ Point.

⊙ Look. ◯ Trace. 🗩 Say.

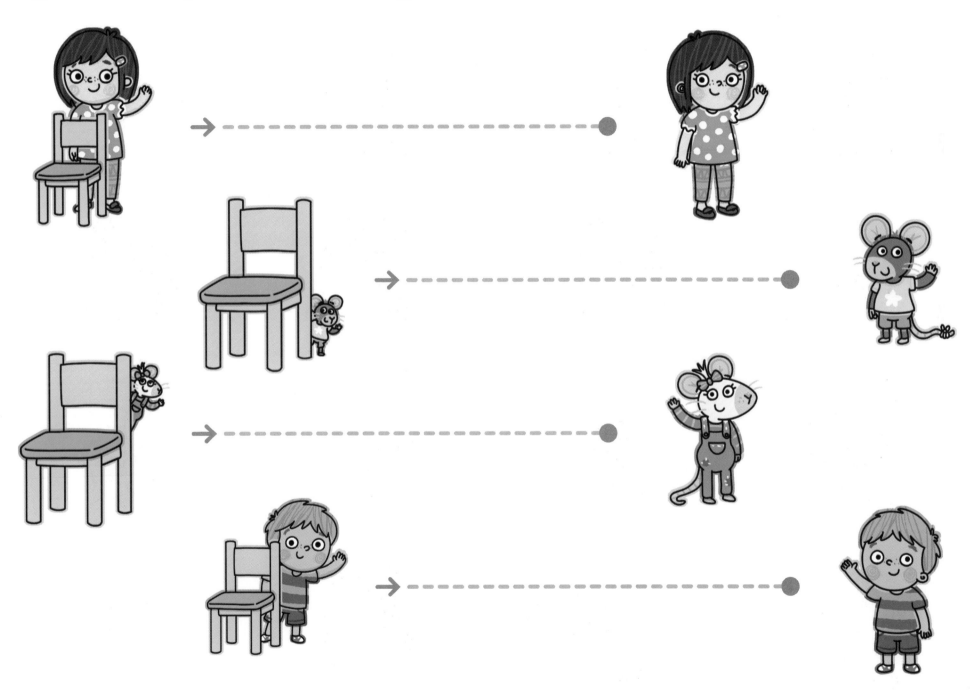

Look. Find. Trace. Say.

1 Language practice: *Hello. I'm (Pippa / Pop / Dan / Kim).*

🎧 **6 Listen again.** 👁 **Look.** ⭕ **Trace.**

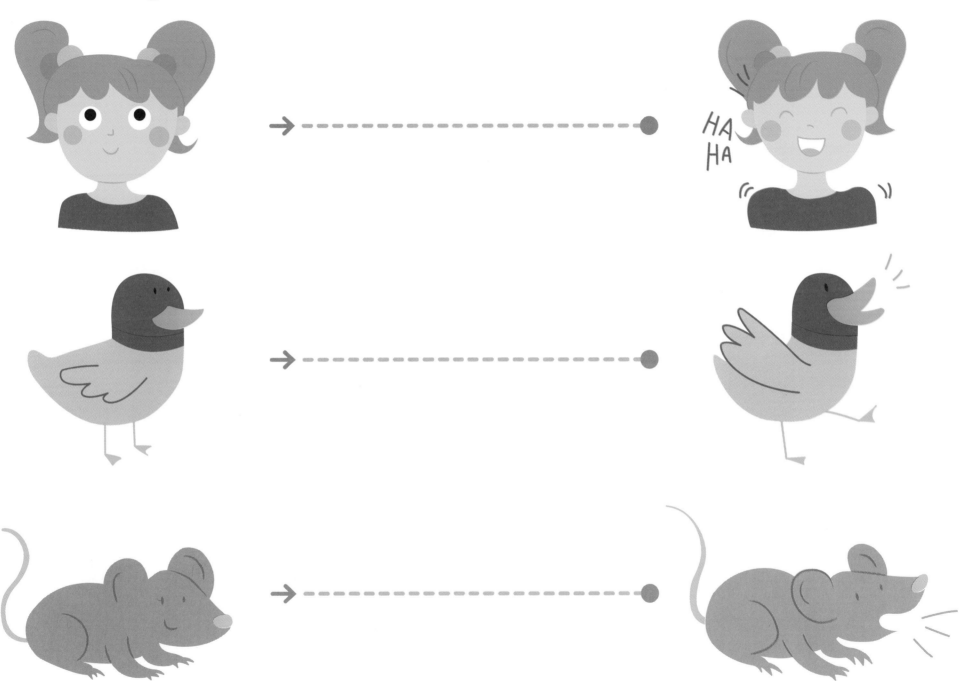

👁 Look. 👆 Point. ⭕ Trace.

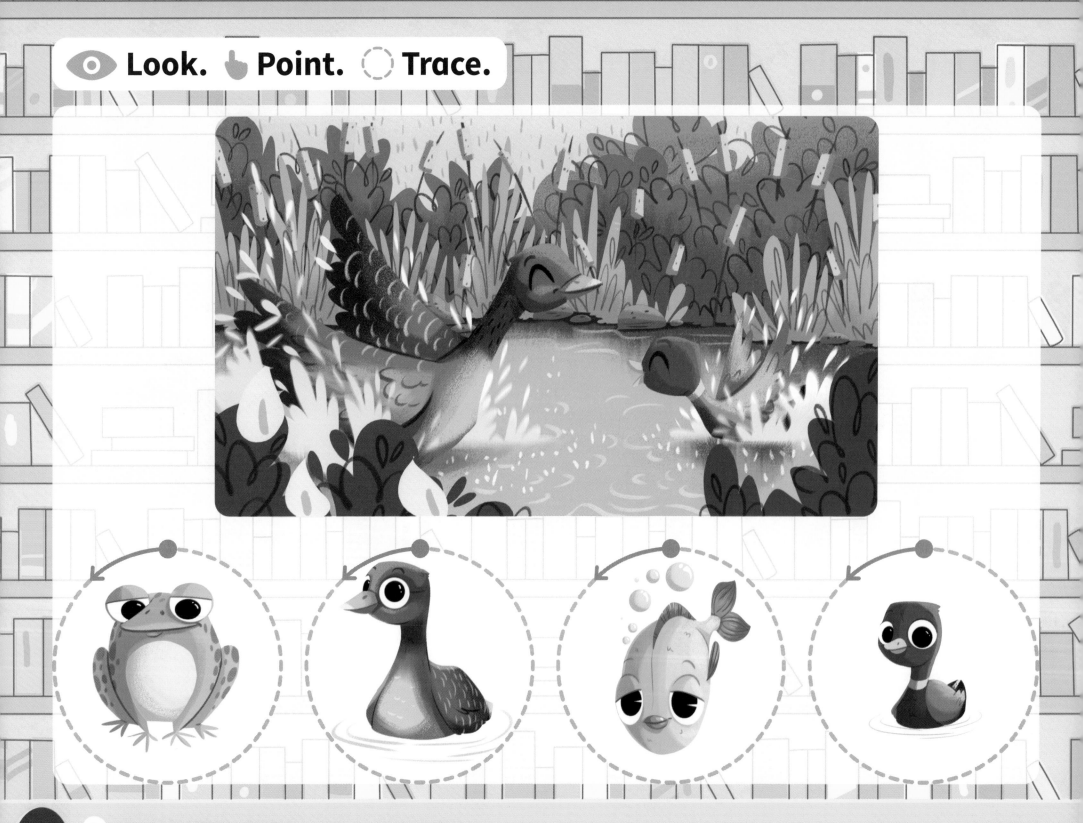

Look. Find. Colour.

At home

How are you friendly?

👁 Look. ◌ **Trace.** ✏️ **Colour.** 💬 **Say.**

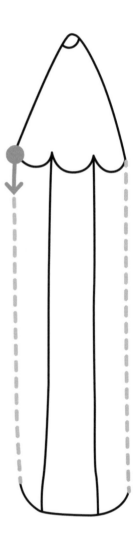

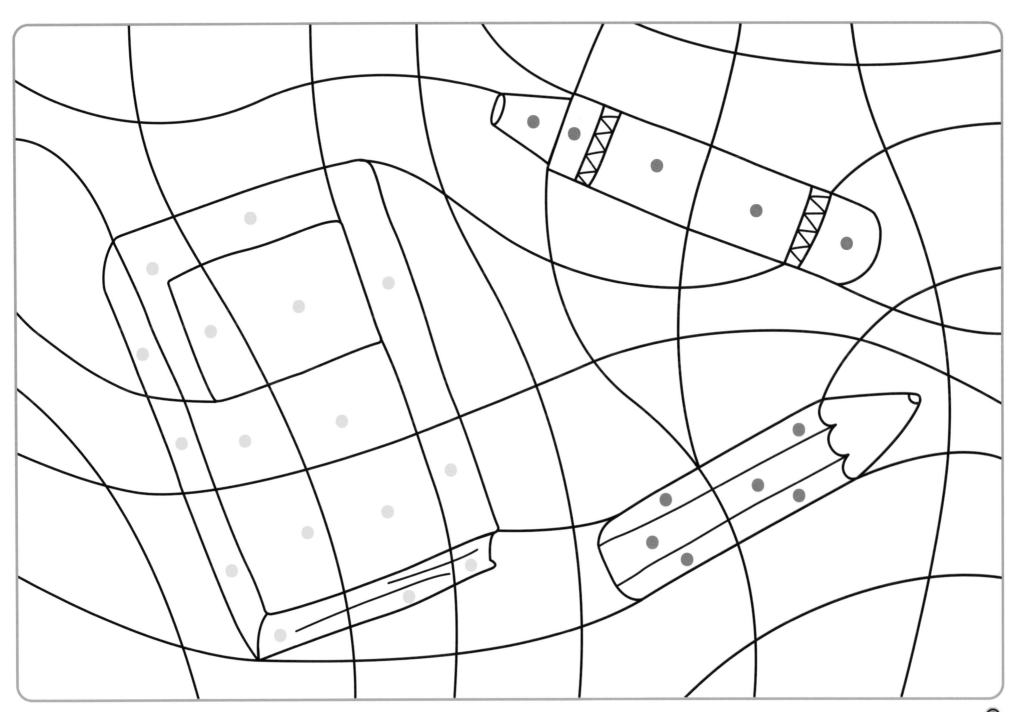

👁 **Look.** ✋ **Count.** ⬭ **Trace.** 💬 **Say.**

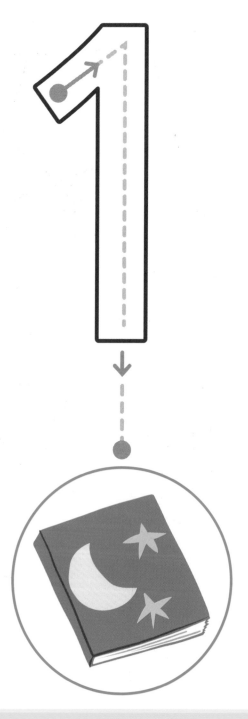

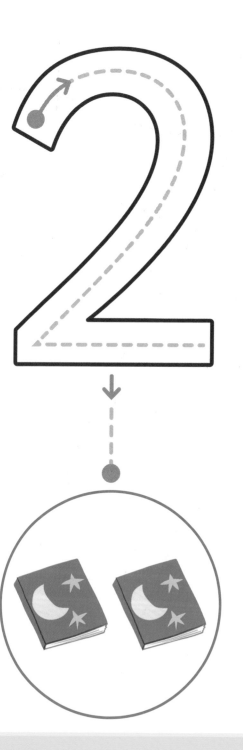

👁 **Look.** 🔍 **Find.** ✏ **Colour.**

 Look. Draw. Say.

1 *Hello. I'm (Anna).*

At home Talk to a friend. Say *Hello. I'm (Anna).*

 Point. Say. Colour.

Well done!

(2) My family

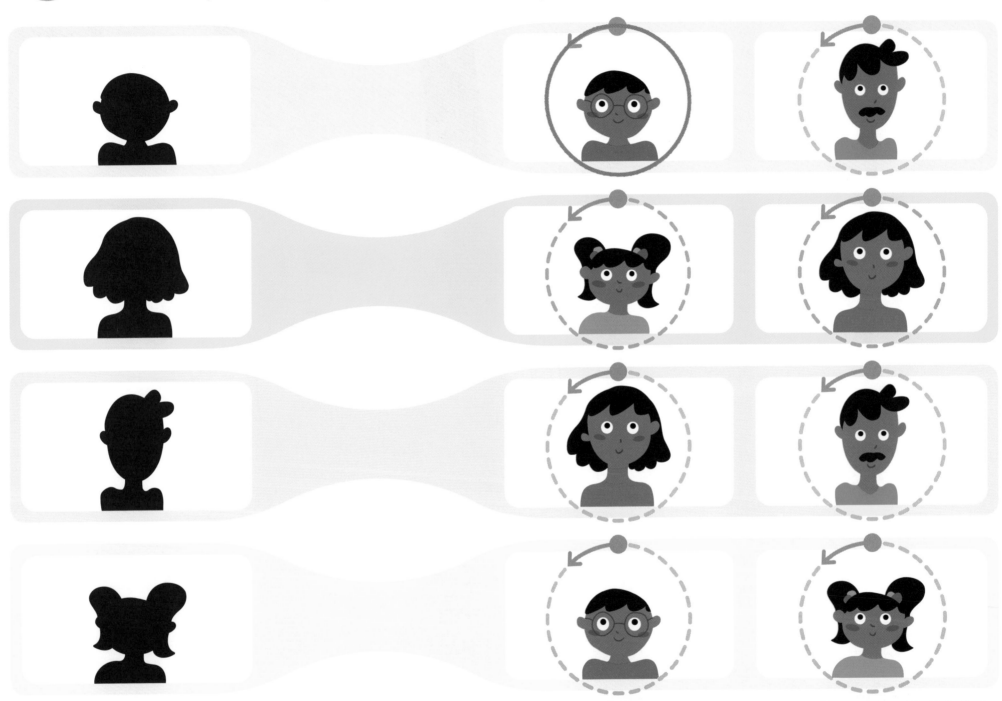

2 Language practice: *He's the (daddy / brother). She's the (mummy / sister).*

🏠 **At home** Find a photo of your family. Point and say.

🎧 **Listen again.** 👁 **Look.** ⭕ **Trace.**

 →

 →

Look. Point. Trace.

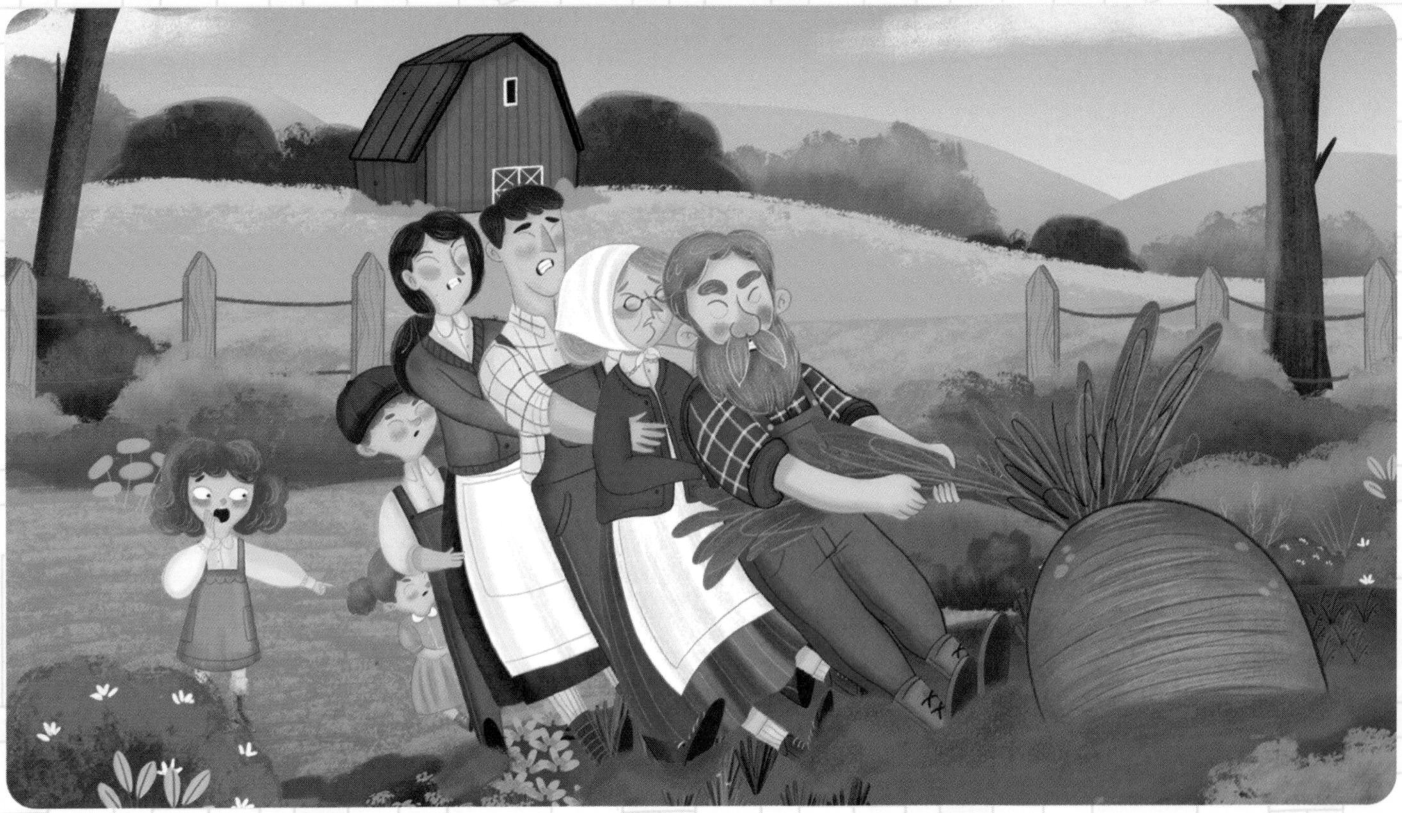

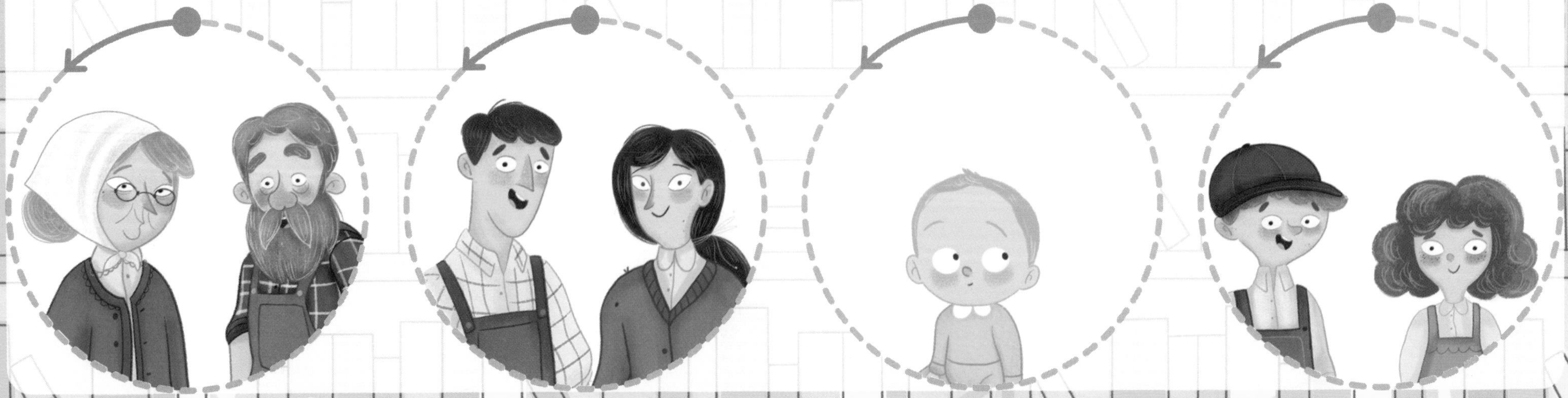

Look. Find. Colour.

At home

Who do you help?

⊙ Look. ◯ Trace. 🗩 Say.

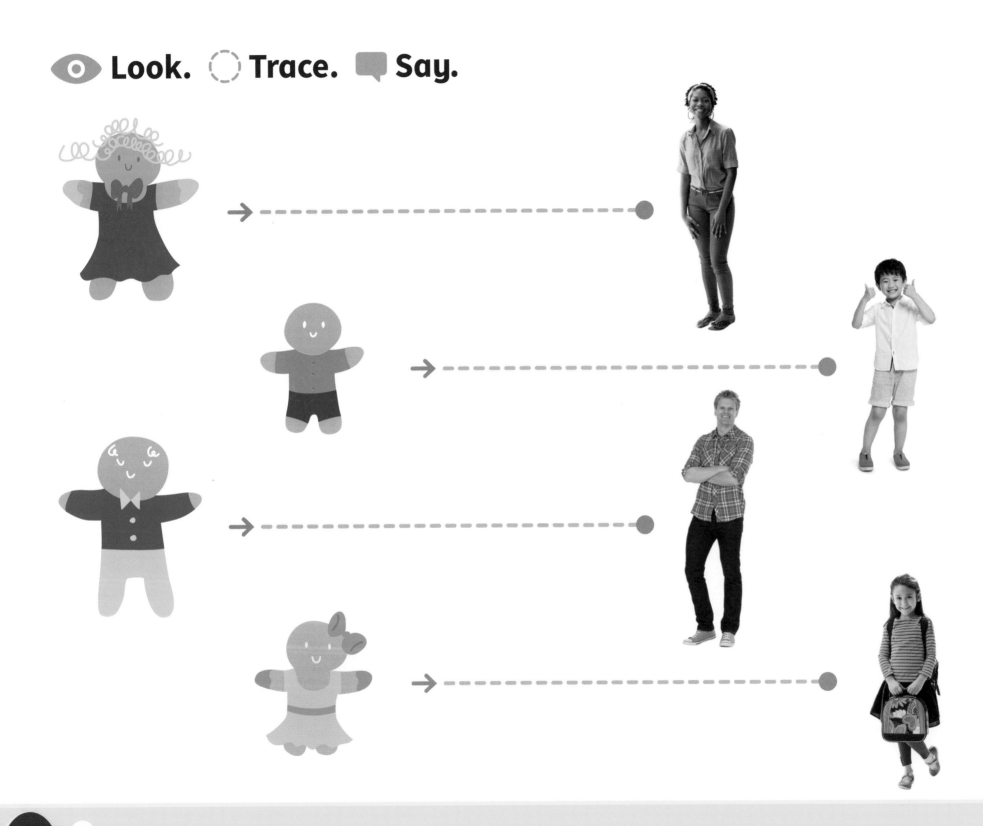

2 **Vocabulary practice:** *woman, boy, man, girl*

Look. 🔍 Find. ⭕ Trace. 💬 Say.

👁 **Look.** ✋ **Count.** ⭕ **Trace.** 💬 **Say.**

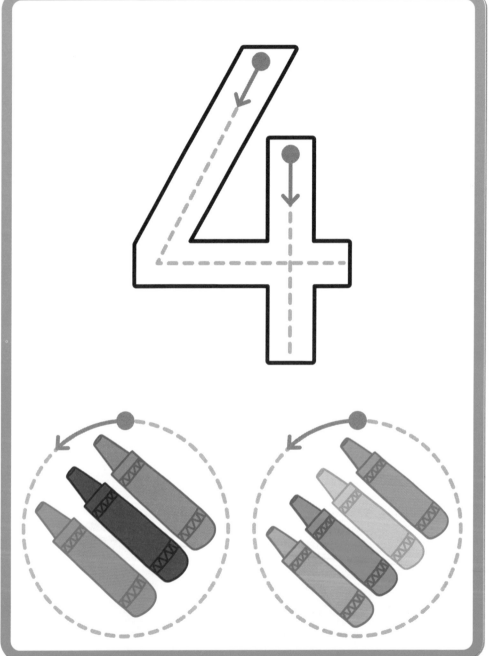

👁 **Look.** ✏ **Colour.** 💬 **Say.**

🏠 **At home** Look in the kitchen. Where is the food from?

How food grows 2 27

Look. **Draw.** **Say.**

2 *She's my (mummy / sister). He's my (daddy / brother).*

👆 **Point.** 💬 **Say.** ✏️ **Colour.**

She's a (girl / woman). He's a (boy / man). 2

③ My toys

 Look. 🔍 Find. ✏️ Colour. 💬 Say.

  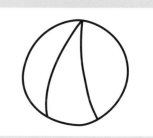

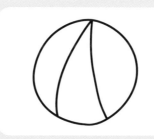  

At home Find a train, ball, teddy and doll. Say.

Vocabulary practice: *train, ball, teddy, doll*   3   31

Look. ◌ Trace. ▪ Say.

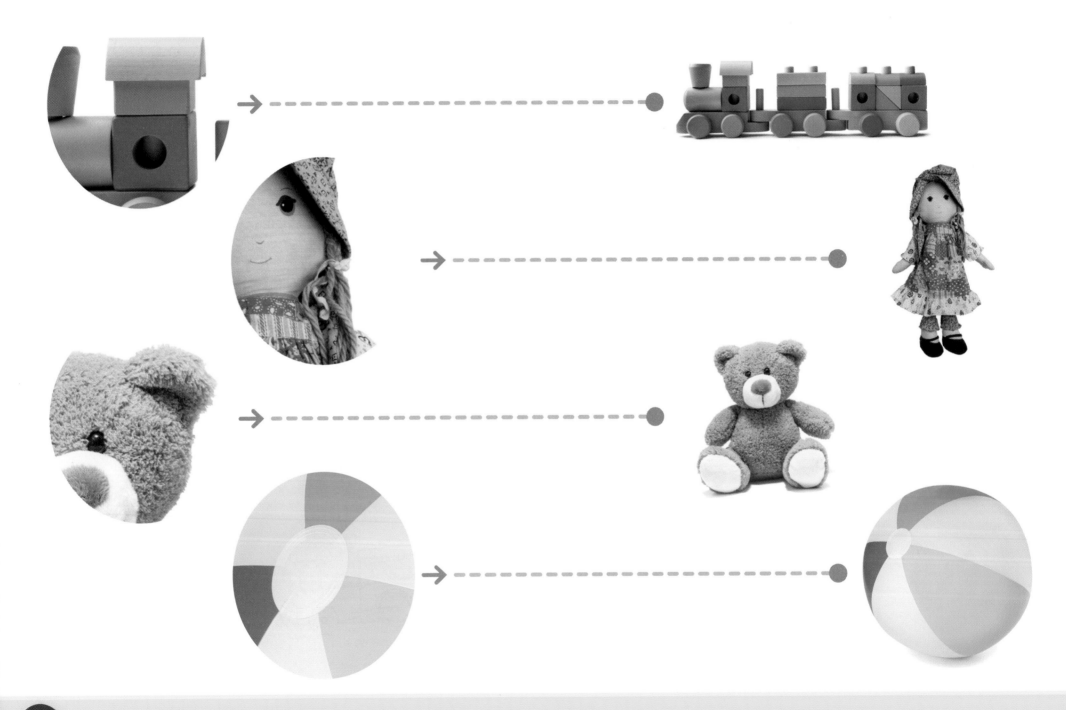

3 Language practice: *It's a (train / doll / teddy / ball).*

👆 **Point.** ✏️ **Colour.**

Look. Point. Trace.

3 Literacy practice: Big teddy, small teddy

Draw. **Colour.** **Say.**

At home

How are you different from your friends?

👁 Look. ✏ Colour. 💬 Say.

3 Vocabulary practice: *blue, red, yellow, brown*

👁 Look. ✏ Colour. 💬 Say.

Language practice: *It's (brown / blue / yellow / red).* 3

 **Look.** **Colour.** **Say.**

3 Recognising patterns

👁 **Look.** 🔍 **Find.** ✏ **Colour.** 💬 **Say.**

🏠 **At home**

Find 2 big things
and 2 small things.

Look. Draw. Say.

3 *It's (yellow).*

👆 **Point.** 💬 **Say.** ✏️ **Colour.**

Well done!

👁 **Look.** 🔍 **Find.** ✏ **Colour.** 💬 **Say.**

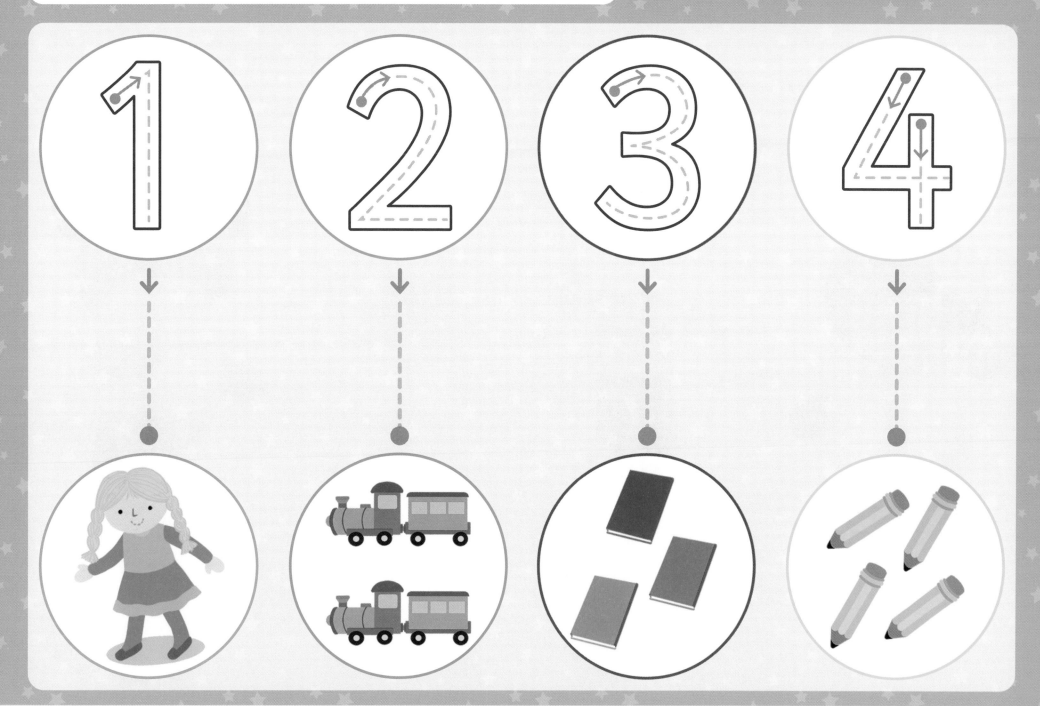

4 My body

👁 Look. 🔍 Find. ✏ Colour. 💬 Say.

4 Language practice: *Touch your (mouth / eyes / ears / nose).*

🏠 **At home** Touch your mouth, eyes, ears and nose. Say.

👆 **Point.** ✏️ **Colour.**

Look. Point. Trace.

Draw. Colour. Say.

At home

How are you kind?

👁 Look. ◯ Trace. 💬 Say.

4 **Vocabulary practice:** *arms, hands, feet, legs*

Look. Colour. Say.

👁 Look. ✏ Colour. 💬 Say.

At home Make a pattern with toys.

👁 **Look.** 🔍 **Find.** ⭕ **Trace.** 💬 **Say.**

👁 Look. ✏ Draw. 💬 Say.

👆 **Point.** 💬 **Say.** ✏️ **Colour.**

Well done!

Colour the (arms / feet / legs / hands). 4 55

5 Food

Look. Find. Trace. Say.

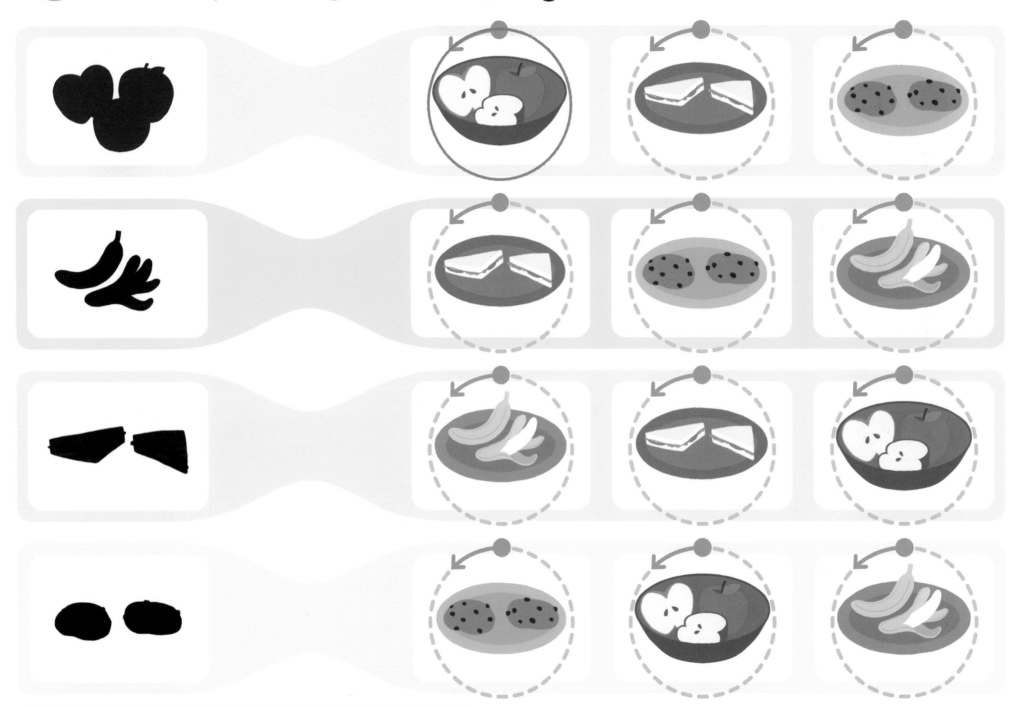

At home Look in a shop. Find apples, bananas, sandwiches and biscuits.

5

57

Vocabulary practice: apples, bananas, sandwiches, biscuits

👁 Look. ⭕ Trace. 💬 Say.

5 **Language practice:** *I like (biscuits / bananas / apples / sandwiches).*

🎧 **³⁹ Listen again.** 👁 **Look.** 🔍 **Find.** ◯ **Trace.** 💬 **Say.**

Look. Point. Trace.

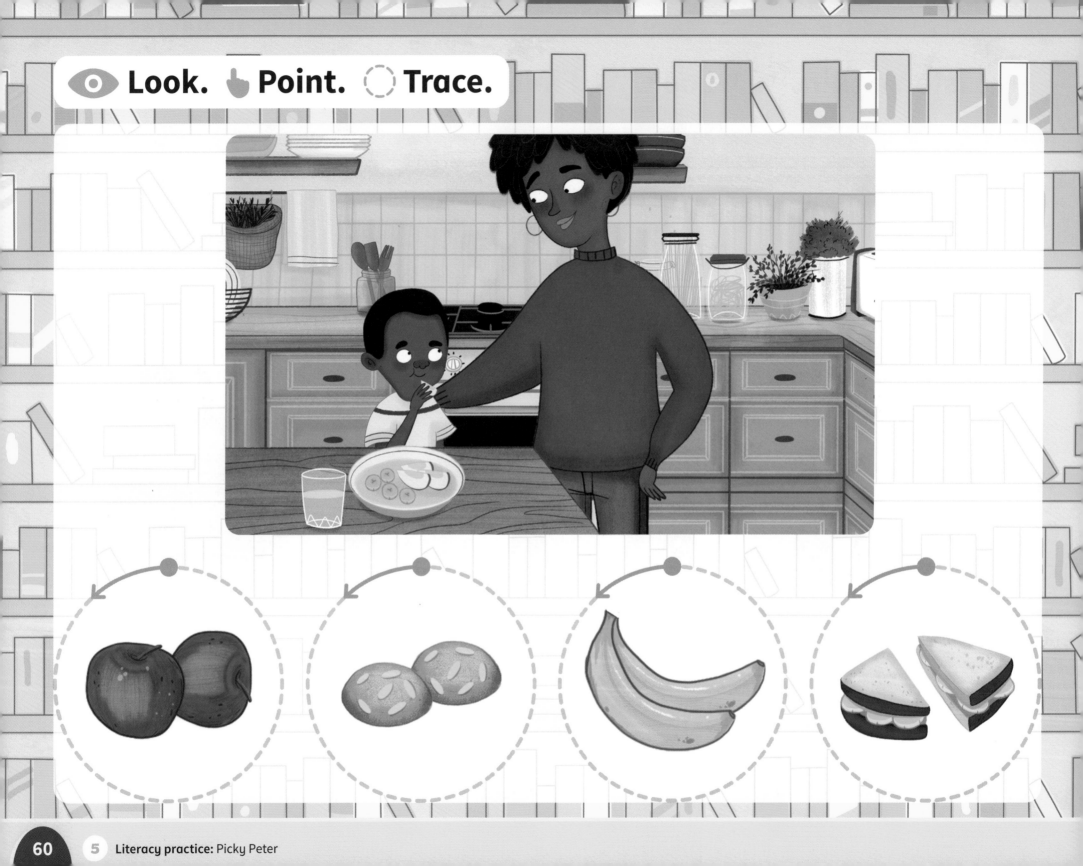

👁 Look. 🔍 Find. ✏ Colour.

At home

Talk to your family.
Say *thank you*.

Look. ◯ Trace. 💬 Say.

5 *Vocabulary practice: juice, milk, water*

👁 Look. ✏ Colour. 💬 Say.

👁 **Look.** ✋ **Count.** ⭕ **Trace.** 🔲 **Say.**

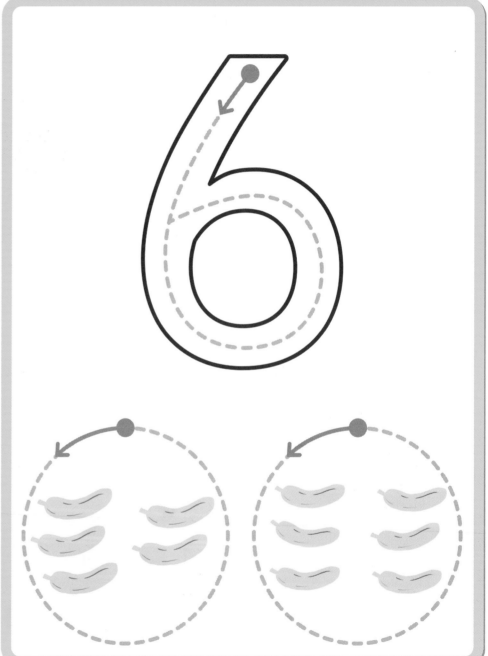

🏠 **At home**

Look in the kitchen.
Point to the fruit.

Identifying fruit 5 65

👁 **Look.** ✏ **Draw.** 💬 **Say.**

5 *I like (bananas).*

👆 **Point.** 💬 **Say.** ✏️ **Colour.**

Well done!

6 Animals

👁 Look. ✏ Colour. ✋ Count. 💬 Say.

🏠 At home

Do you like rabbits, dogs, cats and fish? Say.

👁 Look. ⭕ Trace. 💬 Say.

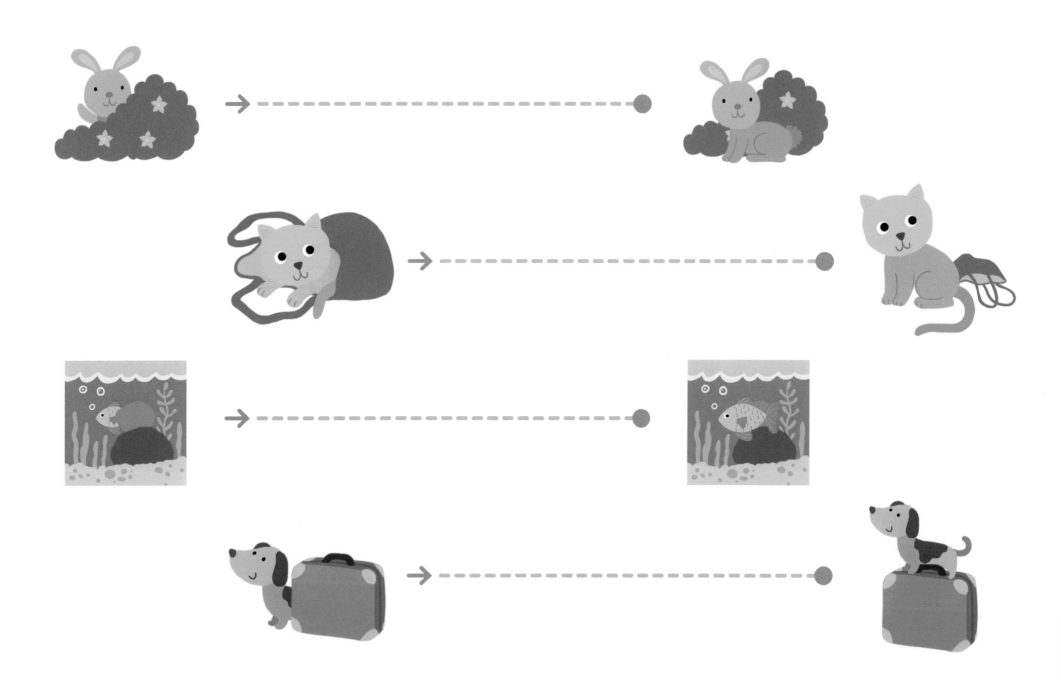

6 Language practice: *Where's the (rabbit / cat / fish / dog)? Here it is.*

🎧 **Listen again.** 👁 **Look.** 🔍 **Find.** ⭕ **Trace.** 💬 **Say.**

Look. Point. Trace.

6 Literacy practice: Emma's new cat

👁 Look. 🔍 Find. ✏ Colour.

🏠 At home

How are you kind to animals?

Look. Find. Trace. Say.

6 Vocabulary practice: *chair, table; on, under*

◉ Look. 🔍 Find. ◯ Circle. 💬 Say.

👁 **Look.** ✋ **Count.** ⭕ **Trace.** 💬 **Say.**

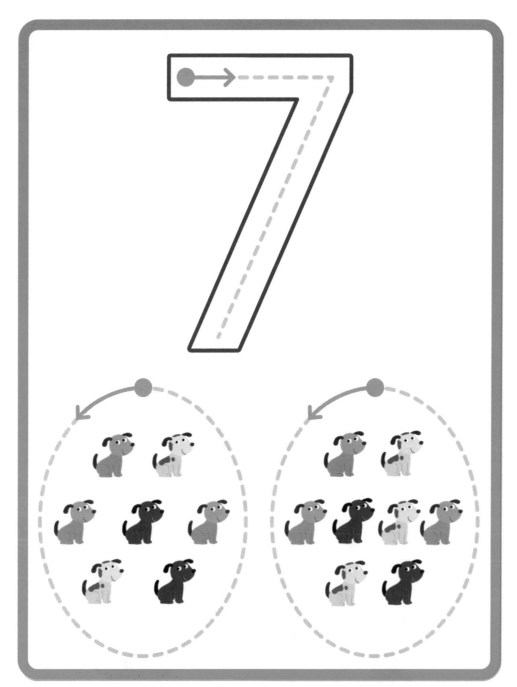

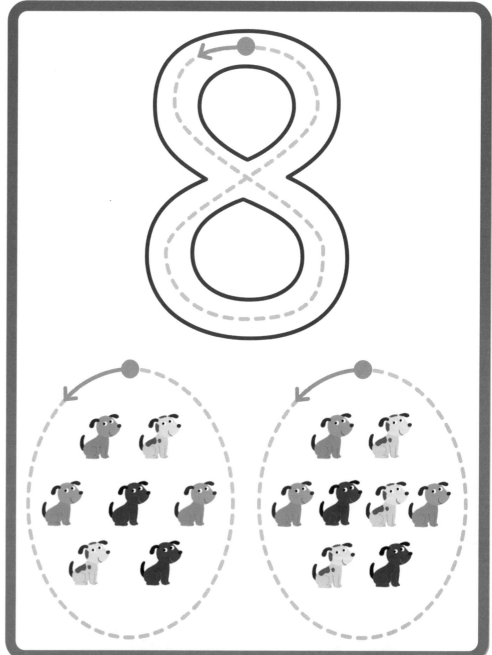

🏠 **At home**   Find a toy animal.

👁 Look. 🔍 Find. ✏ Colour.

👁 **Look.** ✏️ **Draw.** 💬 **Say.**

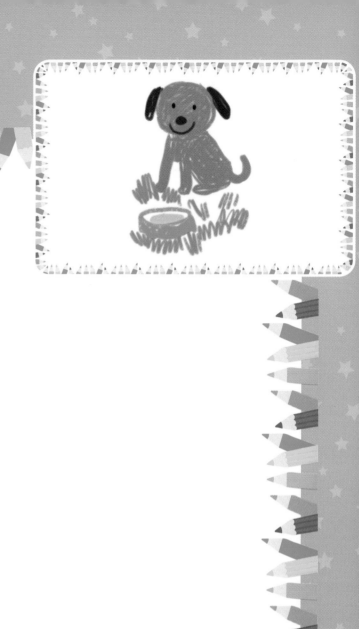

6 *Where's the (dog)? Here it is.*

👆 **Point.** 💬 **Say.** ✏️ **Colour.**

Where's the (rabbit / dog / cat / fish)? It's (on / under) the (chair/ table). 6

79

👁 **Look.** 🔍 **Find.** ✏ **Colour.** 💬 **Say.**

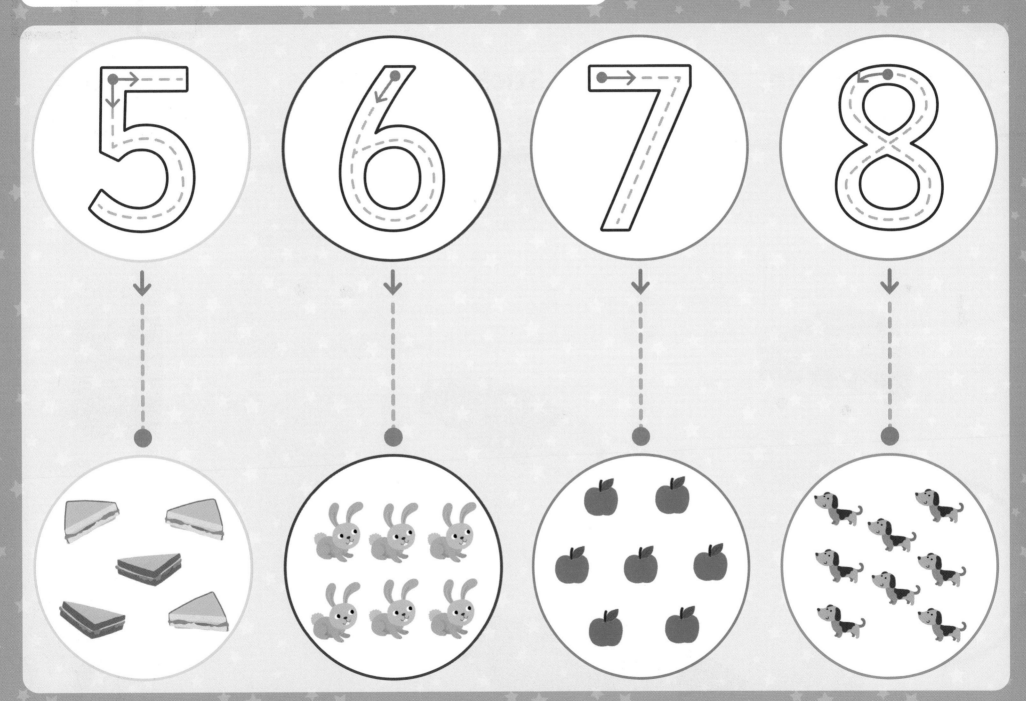

53 Listen again. ⊙ **Look.** ◯ **Stick.** ☝ **Point.**

Look. Find. Circle. Say.

Look. Find. Trace. Say.

7 **Language practice:** *(Put on / Take off) your (hat / socks / shoes / jacket).*

At home Put on a hat, socks, shoes and a jacket. Say.

🎧 56 **Listen again.** 👁 **Look.** 🔍 **Find.** ⭕ **Trace.** 💬 **Say.**

Draw. Colour. Say.

Look. ○ Trace. 💬 Say.

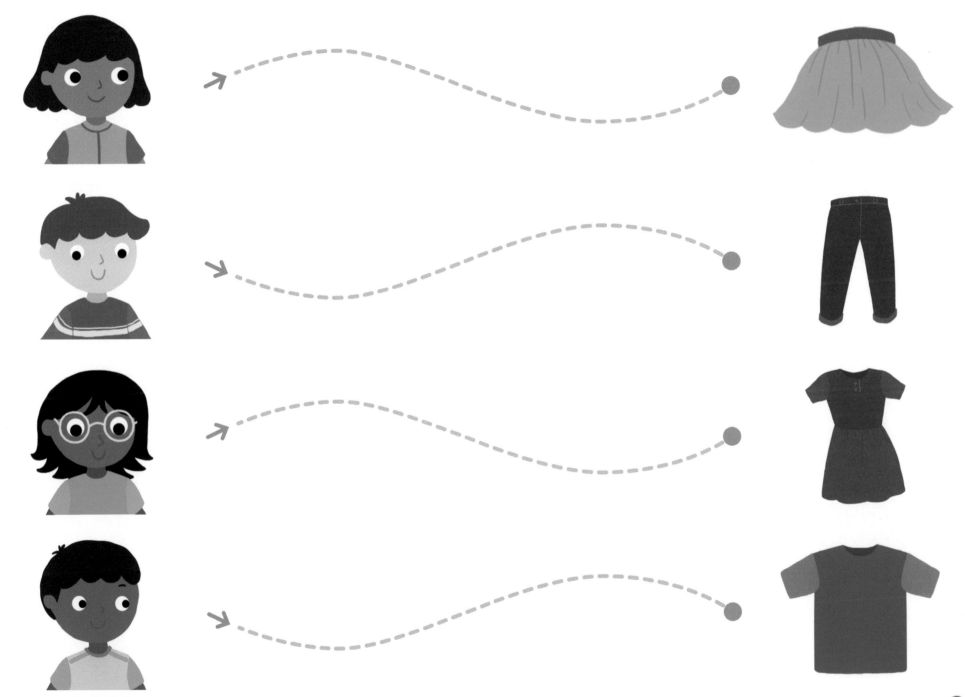

👁 Look. ⭕ Trace. 💬 Say.

7 Shapes: *triangle, square, circle*

🏠 **At home**   Find a triangle, a square and a circle.

👁 Look. 🔍 Find. ✏️ Colour.

Look. Draw. Say.

7 *(Put on / Take off) your (socks).*

8 Transport

👁 **Look.** 🔍 **Find.** ◯ **Circle.** 💬 **Say.**

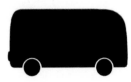

🏠 **At home** Look outside. Can you see a car, a bus, a bike and a van?

Vocabulary practice: car, bus, bike, van 8 95

Look. Find. Trace. Say.

8 Language practice: *I can see a (van / bus / car / bike).*

🎧 64 **Listen again.** 👁 **Look.** 🔍 **Find.** ⭕ **Trace.** 💬 **Say.**

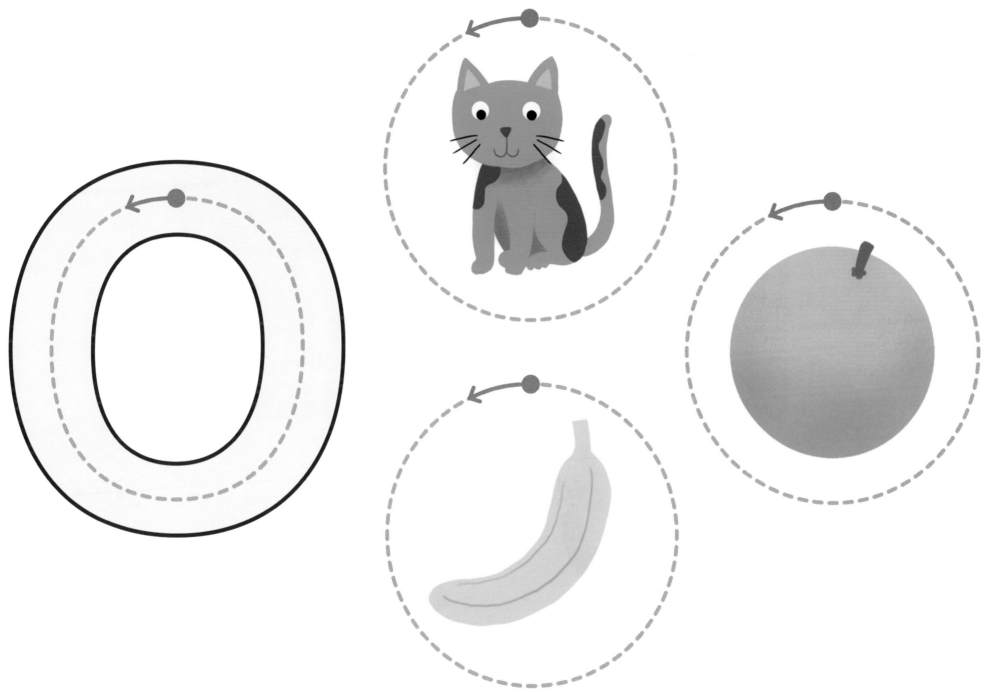

Look. Point. Trace.

8 Literacy practice: The hare and the tortoise

👁 Look. 🔍 Find. ✏ Colour.

🏠 **At home**

When are you careful?

Look. ✏️ Colour. 💬 Say.

8 **Vocabulary practice:** *drive a car, jump, run, ride a bike*

👁 Look. 🔍 Find. ⭕ Trace. 💬 Say.

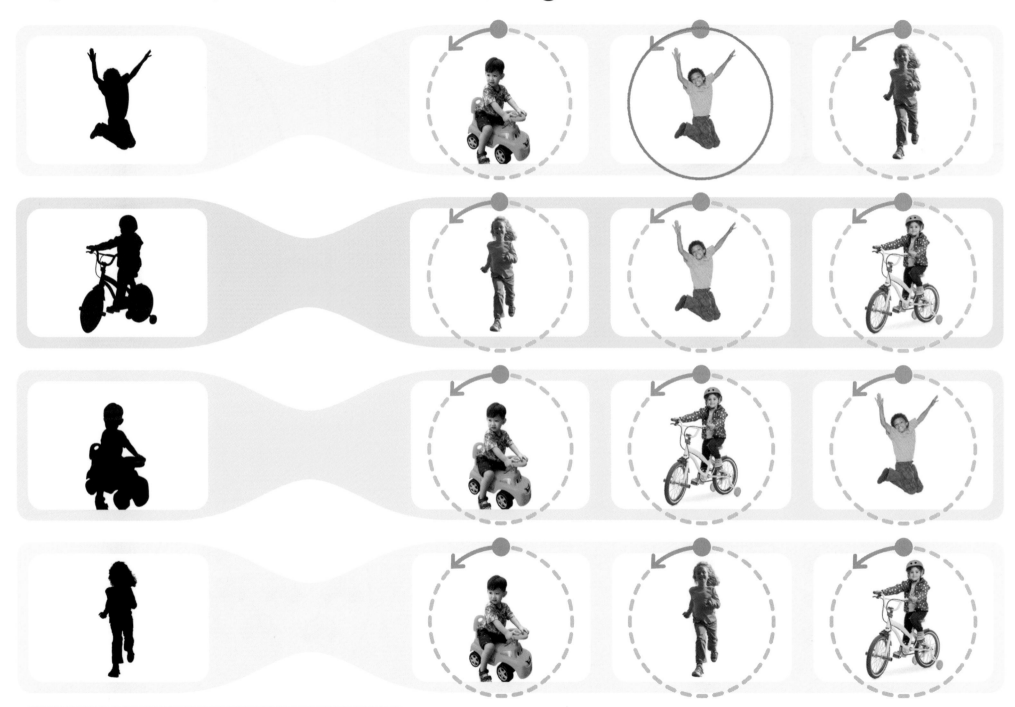

🏠 **At home** Can you jump, ride a bike, drive a car and run?

Language practice: *I can (jump / ride a bike / drive a car / run).* 8 101

👁 **Look.** ✋ **Count.** ⭕ **Trace.** 💬 **Say.**

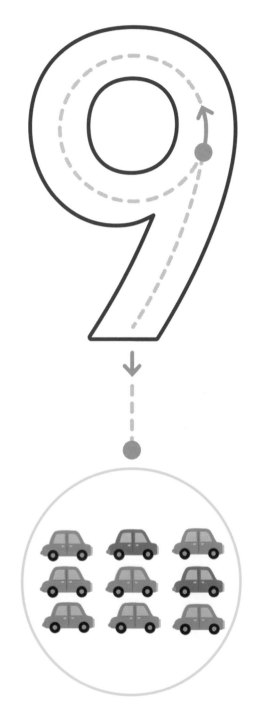

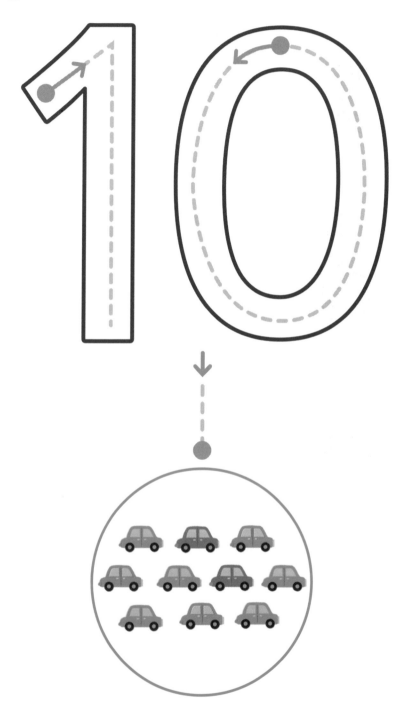

👁 **Look.** 🔍 **Find.** ⭕ **Trace.** 💬 **Say.**

 Look. ✏ Draw. 💬 Say.

8 *I can see a (car).*

 Point. 💬 Say. ✏️ Colour.

Well done!

I can (drive a car / run / ride a bike / jump). 8 105

⑨ The park

🎧⁷⁰ Listen again. 👁 Look. 🗨 Stick. ☝ Point.

👁 Look. 🔍 Find. ✏ Colour. 💬 Say.

Look. Find. Trace. Say.

9 **Language practice:** *a green tree, a brown frog, a blue bird, a pink flower*

At home Find something pink and something green.

73 🎧 **Listen again.** 👁 **Look.** 🔍 **Find.** ⭕ **Trace.** 💬 **Say.**

Look. Point. Trace.

9 Literacy practice: Penny in the park

👁 Look. 🔍 Find. ✏️ Colour.

🏠 **At home**

How do you look after nature?

👁 Look. ⭕ Trace. 💬 Say.

9 Vocabulary practice: *butterflies, caterpillars, ladybirds, worms*

Look. Colour. Say.

At home Look outside. Can you find a butterfly, a caterpillar, a worm or a ladybird?

Language practice: *They're (butterflies / caterpillars / worms / ladybirds).*

9   113

Look. Count. Trace. Say.

👁 **Look.** ⭕ **Trace.** ✏️ **Colour.** 💬 **Say.**

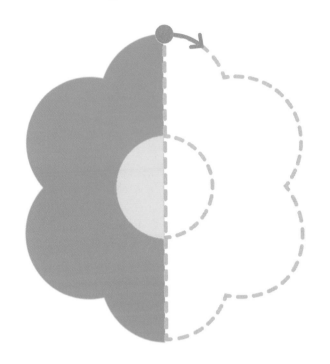

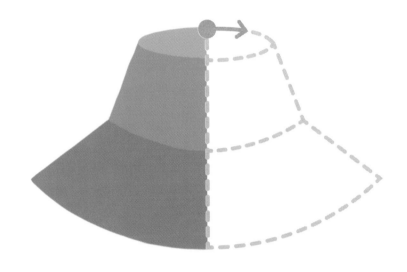

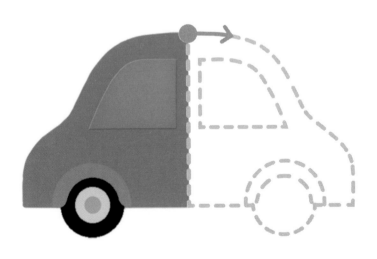

👁 **Look.** ✏ **Draw.** 💬 **Say.**

9 *A (green) (tree).*

👆 **Point.** 💬 **Say.** ✏️ **Colour.**

Well done!

They're (butterflies / ladybirds / worms / caterpillars). 9

👁 **Look.** 🔍 **Find.** ✏️ **Colour.** 💬 **Say.**

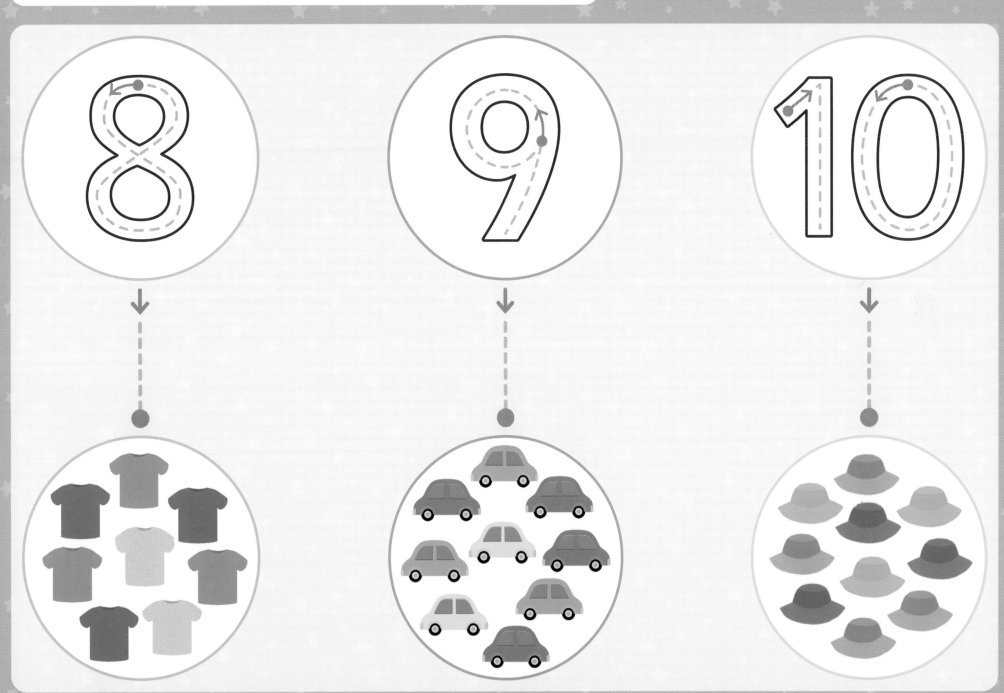

Thanks and Acknowledgements

The publishers and authors would like to thank the following contributors:
Book design and page make-up by Blooberry Design.
Cover design by Blooberry Design.
Freelance editing by Stephanie Howard.
Audio recording and production by Ian Harker.
Original songs and chants by Robert Lee.
Songs and chants production by Jake Carter.

The authors and publishers acknowledge the following sources of copyright material and are grateful for the permissions granted. While every effort has been made, it has not always been possible to identify the sources of all the material used, or to trace all copyright holders. If any omissions are brought to our notice, we will be happy to include the appropriate acknowledgements on reprinting and in the next update to the digital edition, as applicable.

Key: U = Unit.

Photography

All photos are sourced from Getty Images.
U1: Thanasis Zovoilis/Moment; Zero Creatives/Image Source; Liam Norris/Taxi/Getty Images Plus; Mai Vu/iStock/Getty Images Plus; **U2:** monkeybusinessimages/iStock/Getty Images Plus; Jose Luis Pelaez Inc/DigitalVision; BJI/Blue Jean Images; 4x6/E+; JGI/Jamie Grill; Imazins; Mai Vu/iStock/Getty Images Plus; **U3:** Floortje/E+; bbtomas/iStock/Getty Images Plus; Rastko Belic/EyeEm; skodonnell/iStock/Getty Images Plus; Vesnaandjic/iStock/Getty Images Plus; Moyo Studio/E+; Sydney Bourne/Cultura; Mai Vu/iStock/Getty Images Plus; **U4:** Sally Anscombe/DigitalVision; Jose Luis Pelaez Inc/DigitalVision; Camille Tokerud/Stone; images by Tang Ming Tung/Moment; Iliana Mestari/Moment; Victoria Penafiel/Moment/Getty Images Plus; photography by Rick Lowe/Moment; Anna Bizon; didesign021/iStock/Getty Images Plus; Mai Vu/iStock/Getty Images Plus; **U5:** Mike Kemp; imagenavi; Frontdoor Images/Photodisc; Mai Vu/iStock/Getty Images Plus; **U6:** Jessica Peterson; Halfpoint Images/Moment; Helen Davies/iStock/Getty Images Plus; Derick Hudson/iStock/Getty Images Plus; Ron Sutherland/ Photolibrary/Getty Images Plus; jclegg/E+; Kathy Collins/Photographer's Choice RF; Jose Luis Pelaez Inc/DigitalVision; Mai Vu/iStock/Getty Images Plus; **U7:** Jessica Peterson; PhotoAlto/Eric Audras/PhotoAlto Agency RF Collections; Zohaib Hussain; Mai Vu/iStock/Getty Images Plus; **U8:** imagewerks; Tom Merton/OJO Images; Ljupco/iStock/Getty Images Plus; Wong Siewhong/EyeEm; Westend61; amwu/iStock/Getty Images Plus; simonkr/E+; 4x6/iStock/Getty Images Plus; YouraPechkin/iStock/Getty Images Plus; MediaProduction/iStock/Getty Images Plus; technotr/E+; Halfpoint/iStock/Getty Images Plus; Peter Cade/Stone; Mai Vu/iStock/Getty Images Plus; **U9:** Ariel Skelley/DigitalVision; Tetra Images; Petro Perutskyi/500Px Plus; Valengilda/iStock/Getty Images Plus; Flavio Coelho/Moment; Laurie Gresch/EyeEm; mikroman6/Moment; Mik122/iStock/Getty Images Plus;Mai Vu/iStock/Getty Images Plus;JGI/Tom Grill; BartCo/E+.

Illustrations
Amy Zhing; Beatriz Castro; Begoña Corbalán; Isabelle Nichole; Noopur Thakur; Louise Forshaw and Collaborate artists.
Cover illustration by Collaborate Agency.

My friends (Page 6)

 My family (Page 18)

My toys (Page 30)

Well done!

Well done!

Well done!